BLACK CULTIVATION

THE MAKING OF AN IDIOT

Self-help book –

Information with the intention of instructing readers on solving personal problems.

"CAN YOU IMAGINE IT"

Floyd Westfall

Cover illustration by Floyd Westfall

ISBN: Softcover 978-1-5144-9366-3
Hardcover 978-1-5144-9367-0
EBook 978-1-5144-9365-6

Print information available on the last page

Rev. date: 05/17/2016

To order additional copies of this book, contact:
Xlibris
1-888-795-4274
www.Xlibris.com
Orders@Xlibris.com

Acknowledgment

Browbeaters!

I use to think being black was cool. So what happened? When did being black become so nasty and ugly that even blacks don't want to be black no more? How did blacks become jealous, trouble making bullies, that nobody likes?

While mankind is being schooled by scholars and theologians, meanwhile blacks are being schooled by media and jesters.

We mad bro! Shamed, spiteful, and controlling! Must we stay in error?

STOP IT!

Why I wrote this report: As a pioneer, equalitarian, and elder of blacks I am responsible for the common wealth of all black people worldwide. Therefore it is with my due diligence that I work to improve our *image. We must change our *manner, by breaking the cycle of celebrating ignorance. Floyds formula for change: $P={}_{OM}{}^{C}{}_{-1}$ (participation=our manner-ignorance+change).

Why it's important: I want *participation for us! Know this, because of the restraints that we are undergoing, blacks feel more anxiety than is warranted. Anxiety being a constant state of feeling uneasy about what may happen, or an eager and often worried desire, as anxiety to prove/dispute something in advance/beforehand. It is because of feeling anxiety, you will be unwilling to accept this report. Your response being the essence of the restraints that we are undergoing (you have been detached from and made to disrespect everything which gives courage). We lack *courage to encounter our shame. We blacks must face our shame, examine it carefully and stop pretending. Error has gotten us zero, have the courage to admit it.

What's it about: a *Tangent! The surly *insensitive state of blacks! A befuddled people that mechanically repeats and imitates (monkey see/monkey do) without understanding/feeling. The bitter complaint of a black man fed up with being a defeated inactive people, who have developed ways of staying disconnected from real life. Impoverished and tormented, people that spend entire lifetimes pretending not to be aware of their surroundings, making deliberate choices to deceive their own minds, fabricating ways and means to exist there, entranced, engaging in non tangible activities, so as to feel better about themselves. Opposite to sound thought, blacks have a peculiar misunderstanding of conversing with others, in which most conversations are typically misinterpreted and are regarded as an argument. This error in thought generally enrages blacks, commonly evolving into senseless disputes and ultimately leading to physical altercations. In addition this kind of unsound thought is also the main cause of blacks inability to maintain long term relationships and to peacefully interact with others. (According to my own careful analysis and examination, of my own information gathering, and my own personal experiences in the United States of America, and the 120 days I spent on the ground living amongst the common people in Lagos, Nigeria in Africa.) In other words it's about how I see things.

*Image: to picture in the mind; imagine.

*Courage: a union of emotion bent on being fearless and brave enough to accept the realization that we are the face of mental illness, needing regular intensive professional psychiatric care.

*Participation: to have or take a share with mankind in constructive activities, leading to "know-how".

*Manner: a way or method of doing something; personal behavior; a usual way of acting.

*Tangent: go (or fly) off at (or on) a tangent, to change suddenly from one line of action to another.

*Insensitive: not sensitive; not feeling or perceiving.

Foreword

Black Africa

By Walter Lobster

A rich man living in a poor house is still seen by the outside world as a poor man; you see he lives in the poor house. So all his riches, his assets matter not, because he lives in a poor house. Except other members living in the poor house, concern themselves with the richest poor man's assets, none-the-world cares; for there are not enough riches in the poor house to make the poor house appear any better. **It is simply a poor house where poor people squabble over the richest poor man's stuff.** Thus they (all the dwellers in the poor house) are distracted from the earnest work of turning the poor house into what can be seen by others, as a true mansion. The paradise it has the potential to become. The place people seek as a forward destination rather than a place from which the poor are trying to escape. To all living in the poor house, *know that it is the poor house you live in: Concern not yourselves with what a man has, for his true stature can be measured by what he does with what he has to express his Excellence of attitude and his Integrity of standards for his self and his fellow man. Excellence and Integrity: More than just words. When the ideal of Excellence and Integrity become a mindset beyond aspiration and a way of life, they project to be more than a couple of inspiring words or just a positive sounding catch phrase. Entrained as a cultural way of thinking and adopted and practiced as a way of life, the idea of Excellence and Integrity develop momentum such as a force of nature to be manifest into objectivity. Excellent light penetrating mist manifest as a rainbow. In the same way, Excellence of attitude and Integrity of standards, can turn a poor house into a mansion.

Authors Preface

I was scared when I walked off that plane. My plan was to use my construction skills to build a new life here in black Africa. The adventure would be starting from zero. Awe Nigeria my African paradise! Shorts and flip flops every day, 100 degrees during the day 88 degrees at night. Beautiful African girls everywhere. The only fly in the serum, everything here is raggedy and broken. So I decided I would fix this raggedy and broken paradise of mine. After all construction is what I do. I fix things! All I have to do is get back to America and get my co-workers.

I fled America! Furiously angry about all the privileges that black Americans do not have. I traveled to black Africa where I lived among the common black Africans. After four long months, I realized all the privileges that I have in America. I became terrified, thinking that I may not be allowed to re-enter into America. I discovered a new appreciation for my families past, now I know and understand just how fortunate black Americans are. My anger, my fury, have been in error!

I make reference to understanding the gravity of privileges (a special right, advantage, favor, etc. granted to some people.), studying or reading (a book, lesson, etc.) so as to know and understand it -vs- real life experience so as to know and understand it. Two very different circumstances.

Circumstance: L. [circum-around+stare, to stand], 1. A fact or event accompanying another, either incidentally or as an determining factor. 2. conditions affecting a person, especially financial conditions: as in uncomfortable circumstances. 3. to place in certain circumstances, conditions being what they are or were.

> Luke 19:26 To those who use well what they are given, even more will be given. But from those who do nothing, what little they have will be taken away.

Am so glad to be back in the USA!

As I look out my window.

I'm thinking about borders.

Boundaries that my friends can not cross.

For now they must stay put.

Trapped in hell on earth.

Not living, suffering from shame.

And the embarrassment of omission.

Man made conditions.

That wage constant war.

Inside, of our minds.

Life in black Africa is hard!

Disappointment-Anger-Frustration!

I am a very unhappy black man for many reasons:

1. Caucasian oppressors have logically chosen to use all manner of deadly forces to maintain absolute control over black people.
2. Presently today black people are inert, without power to move or to resist an opposing force, with an inertia tendency to remain in a fixed condition without change unless affected by an outside force.
3. Blacks have a false sense of entitlement to be seen as and to be treated as civilized people. But no amount of protest can change the imagination, those mental images of blacks pictured as uncivilized barbarous savages, in the minds of most people.
4. The black youth is terrorized by the mother, everything she teaches the child is done using a whip. The lessons the youths receive from the black mom are chaos, repulsion, very bad behavior, and watching tv. Generally nothing good comes out of the black home, only child abuse, self destruction, and insanity.
5. Black people illogically rely upon magic to ward off caucasian oppressors.
6. Presently black people are unreachable, never breaking character, selfishly existing in unrestricted hypocrisy, always under the disguise of fictional characters, acting a part, whose role is to behave unnaturally trying to deceive. Pretending to be what one is not or to feel what one does not feel, or to dispute what one is or what one feels.
7. Black people intentionally assassinate the spirit of family, friends, and others by predicting the worst outcome of future events to promote staying inactive and inferiority.
8. When others are speaking blacks neglect to listen to the subject at all, are disruptive and very disrespectful, often responding by dismissing the subject all together and changing it to another different thing.
9. Churlish black people never leave home without a chip on their shoulder. As soon as they come around their nasty ugly manner boldy announces "I am angry about someone/something," and as a result "I'm quick to take offense." Everyone avoids them except for other churlish blacks. They begin shouting at one another, "I dare you to knock this chip off my shoulder!" A fight occurs shortly after disrupting peaceful tranquility.
10. I am stuck in idle. Sad and lonely, trying unsuccessfully to rally blacks who cowardly wait for a divine prophesy of deliverance.

Screaming... "What about me!" Why after all this time, I aint got participation? Still, I remain idle, running from the caucasian master. I ran all the way to Africa! But when I got there I did not find us immersed in independence, industry or technology, machinery or "know-how", all

I found were clueless, blind deaf-and-dumb, spectators not participating at all. It's paining me! "The restraints that we are undergoing!" What does that even mean?

Restraint: the ties that bind and the influence that abstracts, as a great mental abstraction; the shackle and the retarder; a restraining or being restrained; something that restrains, as an influence; a means of restraining; a loss or limitation of liberty; confinement; control of emotions, impulses etc.; reserve; loss of freedom, emotion, wit, purpose, will, drive, sensibility, responsiveness, identity, determination, energy, enthusiasm, spirit, the power of self-direction or self-control, the power of conscious and deliberate action or choice, expression, to express ability or capacity.

The caucasian master commands us using words. To understand exactly what is meant, intended to be, or in fact is being signified, indicated, etc., one must think critically, just as he does. You must learn to operate in a like manner or else remain clueless.

The caucasian masters knowledge of semantics, which is the study of the different meanings of words, has allowed him to set up a system of separate commands within a single message. For example: black culture

1. What the caucasian master is in fact signifying or indicating, is something produced by cultivation.
2. What black people think is meant, is having culture: skills, arts, etc., of a given people.

Another example: zombi

1. What the caucasian master is in fact signifying or indicating, is cultivated black people.
2. What black people think is meant, is a fictional tv. character.

Therefore each word contained in his commands, spoken or written, must be carefully analyzed and examined, you must be good detectives. You will need a dictionary for the purposes of defining the intended meaning of each word of the caucasian masters command. Do not and I repeat do not make the mistake and take for granted, suppose, merely imagine, or guess the meaning of any word that the caucasian master uses and do not base it on the opinion of others.

Guilty By Definition

English and American schoolbooks are the standard prescribed textbooks students are issued for a given subject. To study by the application of the mind to acquire knowledge, as by reading, investigating, memorizing, and careful and critical examination of the subject, so as to know and understand it. The dictionary is one of those textbooks that every student uses for defining and the correct spelling of words.

For example the words black and white. According to Webster's New World Dictionary of the American language, Concise Edition. To users of this dictionary: (A dictionary is a standard guide book. It presents words with their meanings, spellings, and pronunciations. Since the language is always changing and developing, the dictionary does not set down rules as to how language ought to be used. It does report how language is being used by educated writers and speakers.

Locating a meaning. "What does it mean?" With most English words in common use, a better question would be, "Which does it mean?" Which of these several meanings serves your purpose-in reading, writing, or speaking depends on the context. Only if you are guided by the context of a word can you find the answer to the question, "Which does it mean?"

Example given; white: 1. having the color of pure snow or milk; of the color of reflected light containing all of the visible rays of the spectrum: opposite to black. 2. of a light or pale color; specif., a) gray; silvery. b) very blond. c) pale; wan: as a face white with terror. d) light-yellow or amber: as white wine. e) blank, as a space undermarked by printing. f) snowy. 3. clothed in white: as, a White Friar. 4. pure; innocent. 5. free from evil intent; harmless: as white magic. 6. a) having a light colored skin; Caucasian. b) of or controlled by the white race: as, white supremacy. 7. [slang], honest; fair. n. 1. the color of pure snow or milk. 2. the state of being white; specif., a) fairness of complexion. b) purity; innocence. 3. a white or light-colored part of a thing, as the albumen of an egg, the white part of the eyeball, the light colored part of meat, wood, etc., a white garment, white wine, white pigment, etc. 4. a person with light-colored skin; Caucasian.

Example given; black: 1. opposite to white: see color. 2. dark-complexioned. 3. Negro. 4. totally without light; in complete darkness; dark. 5. soiled; dirty. 6. wearing black clothing. 7. evil; wicked. 8. disgraceful. 9. sad; dismal. 10. sullen; angered. 11. without hope: as a black future. 12. humorous or satirical in a morbid cynical way. n. 1. black pigment: opposite of white. 2. dark clothing, as for mourning. 3. a person of dark-complexion. 4. to lose consciousness.

So there you have it, presently in the world today this is the image, the picture painted in the minds of every educated person on earth, is that black people are generally bad deserving blame. Opposite to white people who are innocent, free from evil intent, and harmless.

Past & Present Caucasian Economics!
(1st wave of attack)

The Policy!

The task that is given to fulfill is very delicate and requires much tact.

The Mission!

You will go certainly to evangelize, but your evangelization must inspire above all white folks interest.

& The Missionary!

A crafty unit of specially trained operatives, sanctioned by caucasian rulers to commit mayhem and to change with insidious malice, the consciousness of the inhabitants of Africa. Their essential role is to facilitate the task of administrators and industrials, during the robbery of Africa.

A Terrorists Dream

And all the world came lusting after the terrorists dream. The land of the seemingly free, a place where dreams do come true for many. But the high cost of capitalism, the economic system that devours the masses, the common people, my people.

The tyrannous oppressors that continue to subjugate black people world wide, have always maintained their power by introducing terror. Yet within in all of us is an inherent resistance to oppressive, cruel, and unjust use of authority. Not another moment should we stay in omission.

Resist! Singularly Insist on Participation!

Foreign Debt/Strong-Arm Robbery

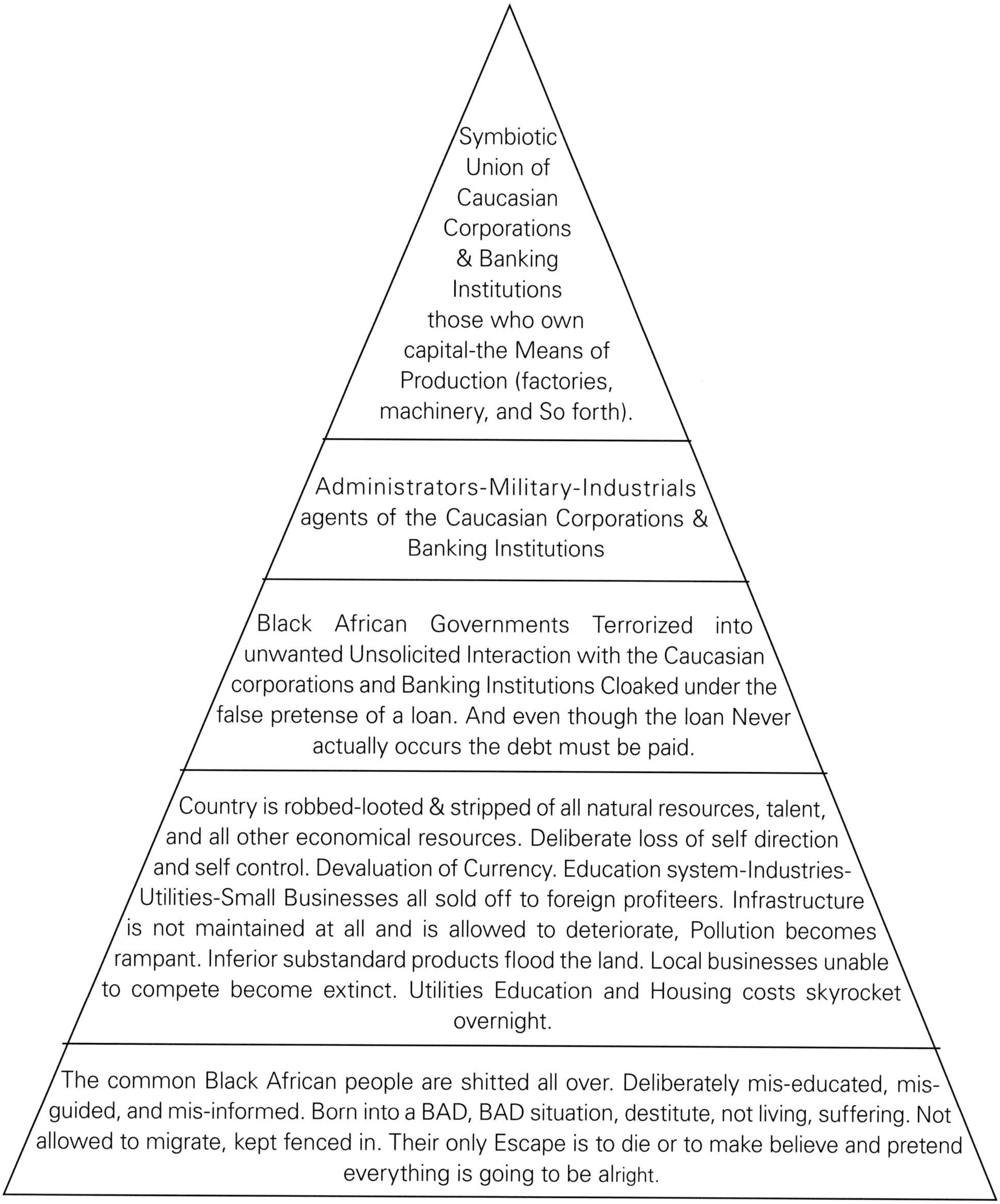

Symbiotic Union of Caucasian Corporations & Banking Institutions those who own capital-the Means of Production (factories, machinery, and So forth).
Administrators-Military-Industrials agents of the Caucasian Corporations & Banking Institutions
Black African Governments Terrorized into unwanted Unsolicited Interaction with the Caucasian corporations and Banking Institutions Cloaked under the false pretense of a loan. And even though the loan Never actually occurs the debt must be paid.
Country is robbed-looted & stripped of all natural resources, talent, and all other economical resources. Deliberate loss of self direction and self control. Devaluation of Currency. Education system-Industries-Utilities-Small Businesses all sold off to foreign profiteers. Infrastructure is not maintained at all and is allowed to deteriorate, Pollution becomes rampant. Inferior substandard products flood the land. Local businesses unable to compete become extinct. Utilities Education and Housing costs skyrocket overnight.
The common Black African people are shitted all over. Deliberately mis-educated, mis-guided, and mis-informed. Born into a BAD, BAD situation, destitute, not living, suffering. Not allowed to migrate, kept fenced in. Their only Escape is to die or to make believe and pretend everything is going to be alright.

STRATAGEM

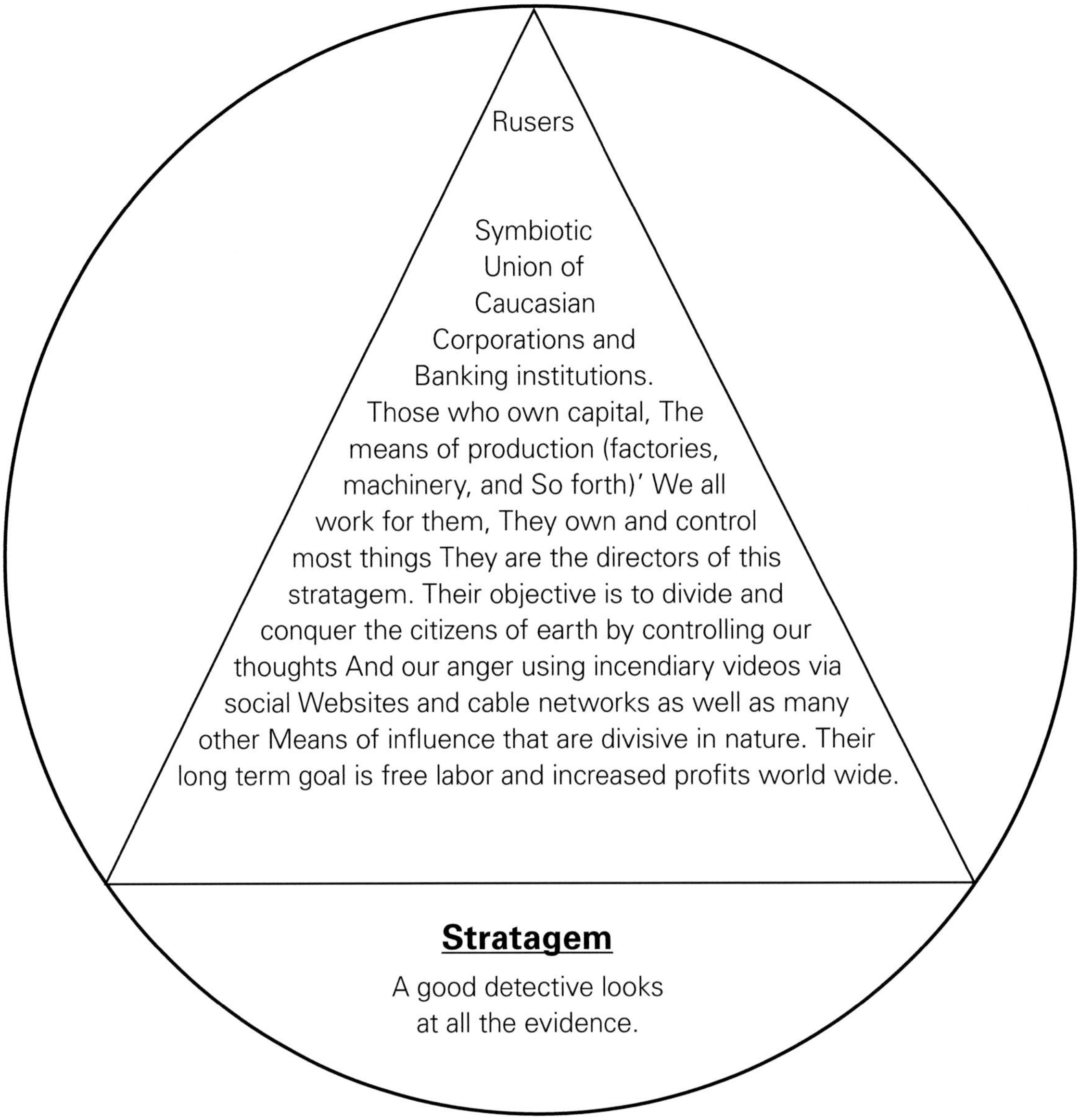
Rusers
Symbiotic Union of Caucasian Corporations and Banking institutions. Those who own capital, The means of production (factories, machinery, and So forth)' We all work for them, They own and control most things They are the directors of this stratagem. Their objective is to divide and conquer the citizens of earth by controlling our thoughts And our anger using incendiary videos via social Websites and cable networks as well as many other Means of influence that are divisive in nature. Their long term goal is free labor and increased profits world wide.
Stratagem
A good detective looks at all the evidence.

Citizens of Earth

This is a set-up, we have all been tricked into fighting with one another. We are the citizens, of earth! We are not: The police, the blacks, the whites, the natives, the immigrants, the rich, the poor, the republicans, the democrats, or even the corporations and banking institutions. Do not comply, we must resist the rusers divisive influence. Failure to do so will result in the continued loss of our rights, jobs, and liberties. We must find ways to recognize one another as fellow members of society. Our union is our strength, without it we will all fall down. Stop fighting and go home. Please! Why go to war against yourself?

Whose Who!

Them Oppressors	Us (all races) Citizens of Earth
Symbiotic union of Caucasian corporations and banking institutions only.	The masses of people common folks, (all races), entertainers, athletes, poor, rich, wealthy entrepreneurs, local-state-federal government, armed forces, national guard, coast guard, police department.

Both of our ails is the interaction or dilemma between those (them) who own capital-the means of production (factories, machinery, and so forth) and those (us) who do not, and therefore are compelled to sell our services in the form of labor to them the owners.

What's at stake?

Them	US
Self preservation and the ability to maintain their lifestyle.	Desire and want to know what good is.

Fixing or resolving this matter depends on ones own perception of what is considered to be acceptable conditions of life. We are all headed for self destruction. Why destroy ourselves?

These are my instructions to the corporations, the banking institutions, and the citizens of earth. Find a way to roll back profits, costs, and wages to the 1950's or 1960's. Find a way to bring back more services and more product for less money. Find a way to maintain those numbers until the end of time. Find a way to enlighten all mankind.

Ecc. 7:17 Don't be too wicked, neither be a fool! Why die before your time?

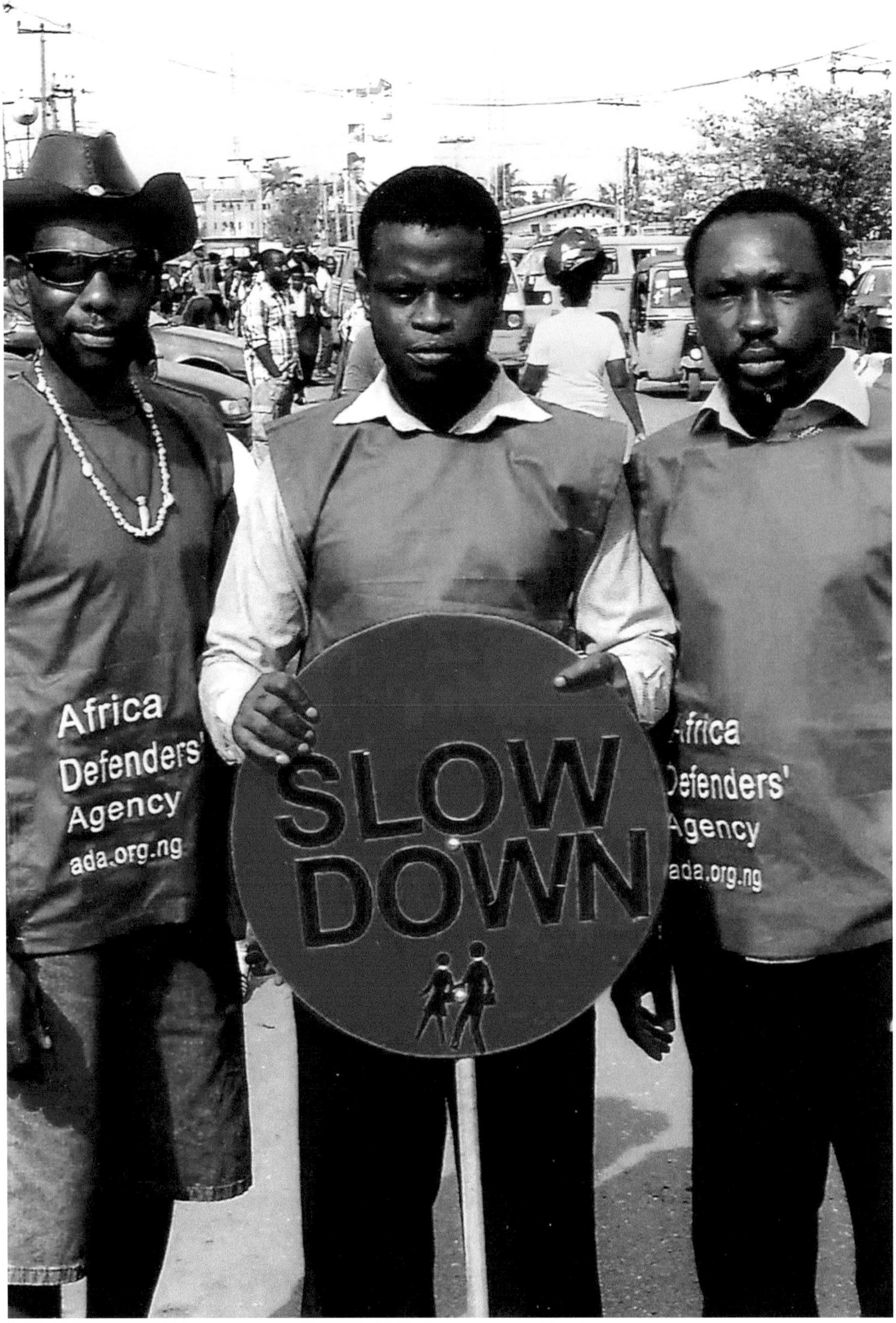
Africa
Defenders'
Agency
ada.org.ng
SLOW
DOWN
Defenders'
Agency
ada.org.ng

God's Psychedelic Doctrine & Me!

Teach a student to read and not to reason will lead to one thing, insanity!

Dear fellow blacks, Gaining inclusion is not free, nor can it be obtained by pretense, it requires earnest work. "Singularly Insist on Participation!"

The statement below is essentially the prime cause of extreme changes in the conscious mind of blacks, as hallucinations, delusions, etc.

1883 (Operation Rob and Loot the Blacks)

Reverends, fathers and compatriots: Evangelize the blacks so that they stay forever in submission to white folks, so they never revolt against the restraints they are undergoing. Your action will be essentially directed to the younger ones. The children have to learn to obey what the missionary recommends who is the father of their soul. You must singularly insist on their total submission and obedience, avoid developing the *spirit in the schools, teach the students to read and not to reason.

*spirit: the thinking, feeling part of a man; mind; intelligence; life will; thought, etc.

We Are Confounded Freedom Is Combated!

Jobs, education, and black history have long been hailed as our newly found saviors but like god they have not saved or even remotely motivated blacks to unite for our common wealth. Education, it's a gag, the pretense of a high position, an artful dodge of trickery used to pacify and to deceive black people into believing there are jobs and careers awaiting them. Black history, in the way that it is being used by blacks, is also an artful dodge of trickery that promotes unsound backward attention, opposite to sound thinking. It is certainly unfertile, having no productive value at all! And then there's jesus, now you have to be a special kind of stupid to continue to worship and pray to the very same white image that enslaved our ancestors.

Know thyself! The black has been made an idiot, a mentally deficient, very foolish and stupid people. Have the courage to admit it. Presently black behavior is to never under any circumstances admit error, always disrupt peace, fight, argue, disagree, and call one another names constantly, no earnest work towards our best interests is ever completed. In fact the only thing blacks can commonly agree on is causing harm to one another, especially whipping our defenseless black children. So I concluded that we are confounded. Unbecoming an idiot would require freedom, that being something which blacks strongly fight against. It is the essence of our present state of being, which is the lowest classification of all mankind. So I concluded that freedom is combated. Thats what the black is today. But we were'nt always this way. Let me explain. Please!

The Cause!

You see, in the run up to war against Africa, in order to increase complicity, past caucasian rulers had to demonize the people who inhabited the land. We were described as evil, deserving blame. And so began our long descent into the shameful horrors of life as slaves. Today all these years later, the war against Africa is hidden, cloaked in many different disguises.

The Effect!

After more than 500 years of war and servitude we have become a race of shamed lunatics with huge egos. Huge egos? I know right! It don't make sense! But that's what insanity is, extreme senselessness! Example 1.) sagging pants. 2.) hiding ones own hair. 3.) referring to one another as nigga and bitch. 4.) hatred of ones own race and self. 5.) fetish (unreasoning devotion) for all other races. 6.) estranged, extreme dislike for one another, etc.. Thus is our dysfunction, we can't agree on anything, we cannot work together, we don't support anything. Living life as individualist, totally mis-educated about most things. Our perception of life is in error, just wrong. "Shame! Our unspeakable truths!" Discuss them, "Hell nawl!"

A Wealth of Shame!

A demon is any shameful occurrence that is an unspeakable truth, and likewise any shameful occurrence that is an unspeakable truth is a demon. Most shame violates what is considered to be just or decent, just the thought of it causes painful feelings of guilt, dishonor, and disgrace. These shameful demons haunt a person, recurring often to the mind and are not easily forgotten, causing constant sorrow. The outcome of such mental suffering typically leads to insanity. A person with this kind of mental illness, lacks rational conduct, exhibits extreme senselessness, and is inclined to foolish beliefs. For example, in the minds of most black people, any non-black person, business, service provider, media outlet, internet search engine, etc., is god. In other words god is a demon. In our case god being any non-black person or thing deified or excessively honored and admired. Another example, a black child is suspended from school for fighting, the mom is summoned and arrives to take the child home. Once in the home, the child is mentally, physically, and verbally abused. The moms reasoning for her harsh response, 1.) the child must surrender all signs and thoughts of free will, to a higher authority. 2.) the child must conform by showing that he or she is obedient, timid, docile, well behaved, predictable, and can be trusted to follow rules. 3.) finally the child must be taught that he or she is of less importance than their mom. This kind of evil terrorism is excessively practiced in the black home. Children are senselessly abused causing mental illness among most if not all black children worldwide. It is morally bad or wrong, unhealthy, and causes life-long harm. By the time the children reach adulthood their behavior is disorderly, unruly, foolish, mad, and totally insane. They go on to misguide children and grandchildren the wrong way. Chaos and insanity is all that they produce.

Why Is The Working Class World So Angry With Blacks?

1. Our manner: repulsive, arrogant, snobbish, negligent, demeanor.
2. Because we neglect change.
3. Because we neglect conduct.
4. Because we disturb peace.
5. Because we don't have solidarity.
6. Because we don't stand for anything.
7. Because we glorify and celebrate ignorance.
8. Because we are pitiful, often arousing feelings of contempt and loathing.
9. Because we always have an excuse for our bullshit bad behavior.
10. Because we immigrate to their countries and compete for their resources.
11. Because we meddle in world state of affairs while black Africa lies in complete ruin, unable to do for self at all.
12. Because we don't show them respect.
13. Because we rudely trespass on their sense of entitlement.
14. Because we neglect their feelings.
15. Because we neglect their struggle.
16. Because we neglect their complaints.
17. Because we invade their space.
18. Because we compete for their jobs.
19. Because we make ridiculous claims to their accomplishments.
20. Because we erroneously worship their god.

Ignorant Things That Blacks Are Proud Of!

1. Child abuse (whipping and terrorizing black children)
2. Ridiculing others
3. Calling one another names
4. Odd children's names
5. False heartedness
6. Continued persistent belief in trickery (religion, spirituality, magic, tradition, culture, heritage, education, black history, shooting or setting blacks on fire, racism, looking and thinking backward, deifying media and jesters)
7. Role playing
8. Looking ridiculous
9. Bad behavior
10. Defending bad behavior

Black people fight new ideas, then defend old fashion ideas by making ridiculous claims that they are in fact tradition, heritage, and culture.

Examples:

1. Non-physical discipline vs. physical discipline
2. Electricity vs. no electricity (blacks living abroad out of Africa making ridiculous claims that blacks living in Africa are better off without electricity even though they have every light, tv, household appliance, and computer turned on in their home while they're making this ridiculous claim.)
3. Blender vs. wooden pestle and mortar used to pound or grind food.

Practice Change/Manners Are Free

Make a deliberate choice to change your conscious mind. The world is not better when you make believe, bad things happen, like getting kicked off a train. Get professional help please!

Suppress the impulse to fight against freedom: (to give the light of knowledge to; free from ignorance, prejudice, superstition, and mysticism). Though it is almost impossible for an idiot to change, never the less we must try.

Recognize and correct your bad behavior.

Suppress the impulse to interrupt others when they are speaking.

Suppress the impulse to crack jokes and mock others.

Suppress the impulse to justify your bullshit, recognize and stop it.

Suppress the impulse to disagree and then get strung out defending your bullshit point of view.

Suppress the impulse to call one another names all the time especially your children.

Suppress the impulse to argue, lie, and then fight when you're wrong about something.

Suppress the impulse to interfere with others all the time, cover your mouth and be still.

Suppress the impulse to find fault in blacks all the time.

Suppress the impulse to talk badly about blacks all the time.

Suppress the impulse to treat blacks badly all the time especially your children.

Suppress the impulse to believe in magic like god which is some made up bullshit especially jesus who is white, admit that.

Suppress the impulse to argue all the time it is disturbingly bad behavior.

Suppress the impulse to hide your hair make time to style it instead.

Suppress the impulse to lie and then believe your own trickery.

Suppress the impulse to judge others all the time.

Suppress the impulse to blame the blacks all the time.

Suppress the impulse to feel hatred and disrespect towards blacks but show allegiance, admiration, love, devotion, and respect to all other races of people.

Suppress the impulse to be nasty and ugly, smile and say hello especially to blacks that you don't know.

Suppress the impulse to be so extra especially when styling your children's hair and clothing it is disturbing behavior.

Suppress the impulse to patronize popular places that are white owned and meant for whites find black owned places or stay at home. Admit that you are not wanted. White folk have the right not to be subjected to our presence.

Suppress the impulse to find reasons not to support blacks.

Suppress the impulse to cuss out or beat your children it is harmful ignorant wrong behavior.

Suppress the impulse to behave badly, recognize and stop it.

Suppress the impulse to snoop on your children it is wrong behavior, stop it.

Suppress the impulse to look ridiculous, especially sagging pants or dressing like a whore.

Suppress the impulse to deliberately be fake especially in the club, at church or on social websites.

Suppress the impulse to cuss and fuss simply because you cannot have your way especially in a relationship such juvenile behavior only leads to bitterness.

Suppress the impulse to snoop into a man's business with other women, know that he will follow his nature to explore possibilities. You will be better off to mind your own business, why torture yourself!

Signs Of Mental Illness!

1. Have you ever stated, I am not going to make them rich?
2. Have you ever stated, I don't see color?
3. Have you ever stated, I love everybody?
4. Do you refer to yourself and other blacks as nigga and bitch all the time?
5. Do you refuse to buy anything from another black, unless you can set the price as low as possible?
6. Do you feel shameful and ugly, unless your hair is hidden (weave, wig, scarf, hat), nails done, make-up done, cute outfit on, accessorized by glasses, jewelry, handbag, and shoes?
7. Do you say hello to non-black people that you don't know at all, but you will be dam if you're going to say hello to black people that you don't know?
8. When a family member or a friend tells you about something that they have just learned, but you are not excited for them at all, instead you reply by saying, you already knew that, and go on to give an example of it. Leaving your family member or friend feeling bad and discouraged, as if what they have just learned is in fact of no importance at all, simply because, you were aware of it, before them.
9. When your child informs you of what has been bothering him/her at school or church, you respond by encouraging the child to just ignore it or you insist that the child stop complaining.
10. Lack of understanding how to converse with others. Exhibiting no regard for order, inability to distinguish between right and wrong in conduct. Frequently interrupting others before they have finished speaking, esp. during church services.

If you answered yes to any of the questions above, know that you have a mental illness. You lack sensitivity and the ability to reason soundly. Please! Get help right away.

*Most blacks are surrounded by mental illness. The teacher, the preacher, the gangs members, granma, mama, and auntie all mentally ill!

Improved Black!

The improved black receives regular psychiatric care. Has good manners, is civil, courteous, knows how to act and is able to distinguish between right and wrong in conduct esp. when conversing with others. Is agreeable, pleasant, smiles and greets everyone including black strangers. Is considerate of others feelings and therefore is careful in speaking. Actually pays close attention to others while they are speaking and does not interrupt at all. Refrains from talking loud and laughing loud in public places, shows respect for others peace. Refrains from ridiculing others all the time and from making ridiculous claims to others accomplishments. Refrains from dressing and looking ridiculous in public, e.g. sagging pants, whore outfits, wigs and weaves that resemble white peoples hair, wearing any type of scarf to hide ones own hair, wearing false eye lashes, and cutting eye brows. Refrains from calling one another names like nigga, bitch, and hoe all the time. Refrains from lying all the time and pretending not to be aware of ones own surroundings.

Perplexed!

The purpose of the photos contained in the first part of this illustration is to show what I found to be the Nigerians biggest problem, "their mentality." Which I would define as fuddled, mixed up mentally, and failing to distinguish between the past and the present. Exhibiting a persistent belief in and practice of primitive ways, mixed and lumped together with a persistent belief in and practice of civilized ways. Resulting in a bewildered hopelessly confused condition. When the remnant or symptoms of colonialism are continued to be practiced in error. Chaotic, illusional, embarassed and ashamed. Puzzled with their own identity on the one hand while repeating and imitating the colonial master on the other. Despising themselves while devoted to the colonial master. Treating one another harshly. Extortion and forcing one another to labor for little or no reward at all. Beaten up constantly by themselves and everyone around them in an endless cycle. Living an entire lifetime believing that abnormal behavior is normal and teaching the same madness to the next generation. Mis-reasoning that if the colonial master saw fit to treat blacks this very same way, then it must be the right way. Lacking any common sense at all, we are snared in non-sense. Mysticism, magic, and supposition, interconnected and acted out by most black people in a continuous twenty-four hour loop. Mysticism: vague speculation; believing without sound basis. Magic: the pretended art of producing effects by charms, spells, and rituals. Supposition: forming thoughts, coming to conclusions, making decisions, based on feelings or opinions rather than facts. How incredibly sad.

Now take a look at what I observed the Nigerians doing. And also take a look at what I did not see them doing.

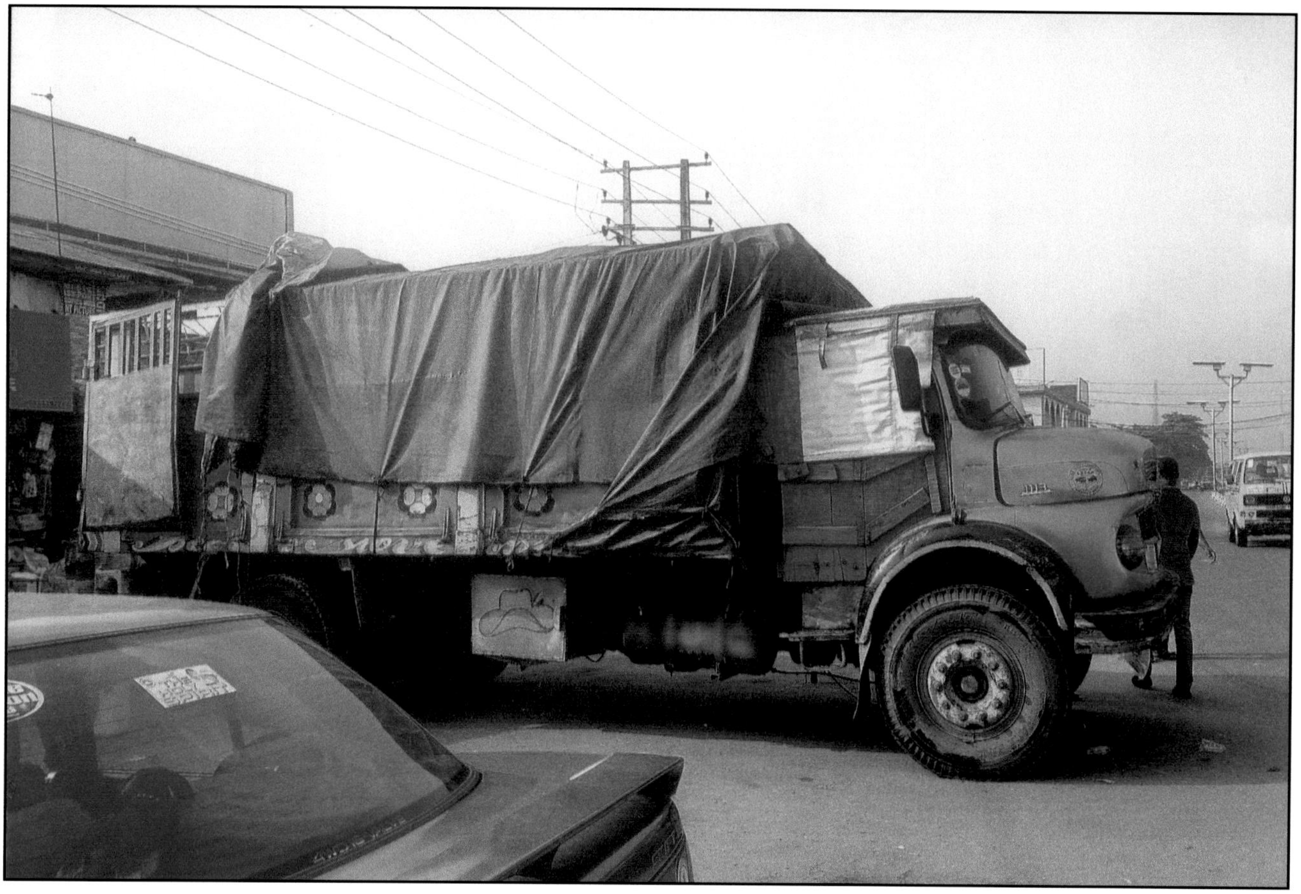

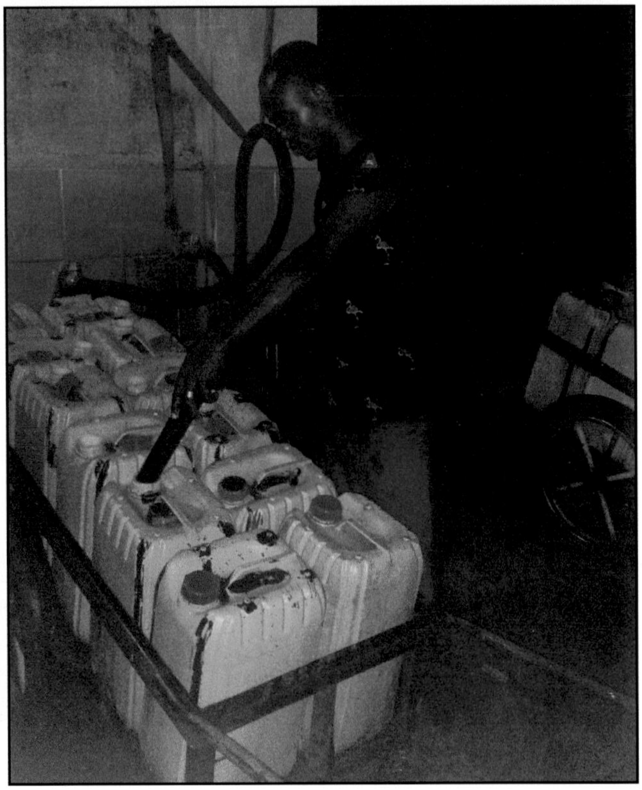

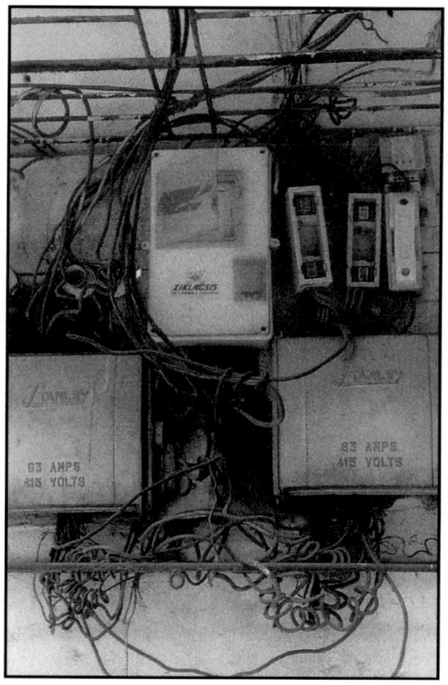
63 AMPS
415 VOLTS
63 AMPS
415 VOLTS

730684

PRO

FREE

Printed in the United States
By Bookmasters